ABIDING
IN THE
EYE OF THE STORM

ABIDING
IN THE
EYE OF THE STORM

BESSIE MACKLIN

TATE PUBLISHING & *Enterprises*

Published by Tate Publishing & Enterprises, LLC
127 E. Trade Center Terrace | Mustang, Oklahoma 73064 USA
1.888.361.9473 | www.tatepublishing.com

Tate Publishing is committed to excellence in the publishing industry. The company reflects the philosophy established by the founders, based on Psalm 68:11,
"The Lord gave the word and great was the company of those who published it."

Book design copyright © 2010 by Tate Publishing, LLC. All rights reserved.
Cover design by Jeff Fisher
Interior design by Leah LeFlore

Published in the United States of America

ISBN: 978-1-61663-975-4
1. Religion: Christian Life: Spiritual Growth
2. Religion: Christian Life: General
10.09.10

TABLE OF CONTENTS

ACKNOWLEDGEMENTS

I would like to acknowledge my daughter, Stephanie, who has been a real source of motivation and encouragement to me. She has always let me know that she believes in me and has supported me in the ventures that the Holy Spirit placed in my heart.

Bless you, daughter, and may the gifts that have been imparted into your life begin to flower and bloom eternally for our Lord.

The Spirit of the Lord is still saying, *"Go through, my child; go through."*

I also acknowledge my mother, Angela Davis, the matriarch of my family, for being that example for me of a woman that has gone through her storms of life focused on God, who strengthened her with perseverance, fortitude, and courage, and with a love for her family and herself.

Mom, I'd like to thank you for being that example of a woman.

INTRODUCTION

I've come to the conclusion that the only thing different from Christians and those that are not Christians is that we have a God that has given us eternal life through his Son, Jesus Christ. We will die just like they will die, but we will rise to eternal life; those that are not Christians will arise to eternal damnation.

We all suffer the joys and trials of life because just living will bring to us unpredictable changes and variations that will continue to occur throughout our lifetime as long as we continue to breathe and walk upon this earth. It doesn't matter whether we are Christians or atheist, we will all at sometime or other shed tears of sadness, joy, and grief. We will all suffer, but to what magnitude is not always determined by us.

I believe that the difference between Christians and others that have not the true and living God is that we have a hope that keeps us forging ahead and reaching and pressing, looking for the brighter day.

Storms will arise in every person's life that is living on planet earth, but how we go through our storm will truly identify where we are on our spiritual journey. Even now, I hear the voice of the Lord saying, *"Go through, my child; go through."*

THE STORMS

I can still hear Momma saying, "You just keep on living and you will find out that everyone has a measure of trouble to come into their life."

I said to her, "Oh no, Momma, I'm not going to have all that trouble because those people made stupid and foolish mistakes and they brought all that trouble on themselves; but I'm going to be wise."

Momma would just ignore me and say, "Just keep on living child." I would just look at her and think to myself, she doesn't know what she's talking about, and walk away. You know what I discovered later in life? *Momma knows best!* Momma knew what she was talking about and Momma was right!

Trouble does find its way into every life and it doesn't care whether you are foolish or wise, rich or poor; sooner or later it will knock on your door and hand you your measure of grief, distress, sorrow, and despair to cause unrest and chaos in your life. Get ready, because trouble will come, and the majority of the time it will arrive un-expectedly and unannounced. It will say, "Surprise! Here I am, so show me my room; I think I will stay awhile."

We Christians have a saying that trouble doesn't last always. This is our way of affirming that it will come, but it won't last. We also learned by just living and observing that the sun doesn't shine all the time, sometimes it rains and not only will it rain, but there may be raging storms. Now let me talk to you about the storms.

Storms can be very peculiar; sometimes they can be very destructive or they can be just loud and windy with much rain and little or no damage. Either way, destructive or not destructive, you can recognize that you are in a storm. They can arise suddenly or give forewarning that it is on the way. Either way, you will know when it has arrived and when it has departed.

I believe that we are always given a warning that a storm is on the way. We may not hear the warning, because we are too busy with other things going on in our life, but the warning does come. Sometimes we don't heed the warning or we overlook the warning. We say to ourselves, "What does that weather man know? He forecasted a storm last week and it passed over us." So we continue on with our daily routine and make no prepara-tion. Can't you recall someone telling you at some point in your life, "Don't spend all your money; tuck some away for that rainy day?" They were warning you that the sun wasn't going to be shining all the time, but that some rain was going to fall. They were trying to tell you that you might have more than enough right now, but lean times will come, so be prepared.

Storms can manifest as one of the many trials of life. What is it that you are facing that is disrupting your peace and calm? What is causing your life to be in a frantic and chaotic state? Is it a loss of a loved one? Is it a dreaded disease? Is it a financial whirlwind? Whatever the storm, hurricane, tornado, thunder storm, or tsunami, you will need to know how to go through and survive in these tumultuous times.

Remember, you have the over-comer residing within you. Jesus said, "Fear not, little children, for I have already overcome the world." He meant whatever storm you are facing, you must remember you are not alone. He is right there with you and he has the keys for victory in his hands.

We have learned by reading our Bibles that we have the power of Christ in us to enable us to overcome all troubling circumstances. I wonder why during times of crisis we often forget who resides within us. The Word of God says, "The Lord thy God in the midst of you is mighty." (Zephaniah 3:17) I have been guilty on many occasions of forgetting that Jesus is right there in the midst of my situation, and on those occasions, I did begin to fret and become anxious about my condition and my survival. I did allow fear to rule for a moment or two, and I did become unbalanced and unfruitful in my thinking because I was no longer Christ-centered, but problem-centered. I would momentarily lose view of the Almighty himself. Therefore, I lost access to his strength, to his power, and to his wisdom.

Our heavenly Father is not a fair-weather friend; he is always there in the good times and in the worst of times. Faithful is he!

THE SAFE PLACE

There is a place that is called *the eye of the storm*, and this is the place where there is perfect peace and calmness, though all around you might be raging, you can find peace and safety right in the midst of your storm.

Psalm 91:1–2 says, "He that dwells in the secret place of the most High shall abide under the shadow of the Almighty."

"I will say of the Lord, He is my refuge and my fortress; my God, in him will I trust." The eye of the storm is God's secret place. It's the place where we can find shelter. The eye of the storm is God Almighty himself.

The eye of the storm is the place where you want to abide, because this is the safe place. This is God's secret place. This is the place where you will be abiding under the shadow of the Almighty. You will find God hovering over you in this place; providing you his protective covering from whatever elements that would come your way. I don't know about you, but I like being in the presence of God.

I love this example that the Bible gives, because if you remain under his shadow, you will know that whatever situation he allows to touch your life in a negative way; you are well able to handle it. You can find strength and comfort in knowing that this is the will of the Lord concerning you.

Everything that happens under his shadow is the very thing that he allows. When you know that God permitted the bad to happen, then there must be a hidden good that you don't want to overlook. Continue to abide in his secret place and you won't miss what he has for you. This might be a closer walk with him, which is priceless. When troubles come and we handle them without vacating our position in Christ, we will discover a dimension of God our Father that we were not aware. I believe that this is where we begin to gain an understanding of the depth, the width, and the breadth of his love for us. God is fixed in his love for us.

The key is to remain fixed in our love and steadfast in our faithfulness to the Father and to bear up under the pressures of life that are sent to cause us to abandon our place of safety. It is not easy to abide in a place where the winds of life circumstances are furiously blowing and threatening to uproot everything that that you have worked diligently for; but you will need to remain stable and unyielding to its destructive force. The key is to dwell there, to take up a residency there.

It is when we come to terms with our doubt and unbelief that we are able to cry out for help and receive his power to endure and withstand the torrential rains of family troubles and job woes, sickness, and disease. When you cry out, "Lord, help my unbelief," then you will hear him say, "Trust me."

Under the shadow of the Almighty is being in the presence of the Lord. We have and experience fullness of joy when we come to the realization that we are being watched over by God and that there is nothing that escapes his watchful eyes. While you are abiding in your safe place, wait for the change in your situation without giving up your hope.

HIS PROTECTION

We have protection in our storms and we should run for cover. Our God is our refuge in the storms, because he covers and shields us in these times. God will cover us and protect from the things that we can see and from what we don't see coming our way. It is a comforting and a consoling thing to know that we are covered and cared for by our heavenly Father. Imagine God as a great big umbrella and you are under him. Now do you feel protected? There is a song that says he has the whole world in his hands. Well, imagine that he is holding you in his hand under his all encompassing umbrella. Don't you feel protected and safe?

Recently, we had a powerful wind storm in my city and homes were damaged by the force of the winds, and shingles from the roofs of the homes were strewn everywhere. Some homes were damaged by fallen trees, but the home owners had protection from the storm's damage. They were covered by their insurance companies. Our heavenly Father is our protection and blessed assurance that whatever the enemy takes from us in the storms of life; he will restore. *You are covered!*

Psalm 91:4 says, "He shall cover thee with his feathers, and under his wings shall thou trust and his truth shall be thy shield and buckler." We can depend and rely on God to shield us. I love this Scripture because every time I read it, I visualize a mother hen with her wings spread and her little chicks are safely nestled beneath her feathers protected from danger and harm.

Knowing that we are covered by God brings with it a peace, serenity, and a perfect calmness to our spirit and soul. We are able to inhale and exhale his breath of life that causes all worry, fear, and anxiety to give way to perfect stillness in our innermost being. Now breathe and then breathe again; now experience the peace and serenity that has entered your body. This is when you can truly say it is well with my soul and mean it.

Nevertheless, we need to prepare for the storms of life so that we will not be caught off guard. Now what is the first thing we should do to prepare?

A TIME OF PREPARATION

I believe we are always being warned that storms will arrive in our life. If we are Christians and we attend church, we receive warnings every Sunday that we need to be prepared. We need to be prepared for our saviors returning and we also need to be prepared for the various things that could happen to us in this lifetime.

We are to be sober and alert so that we are not caught off guard. We cannot afford to wait until the storm has arrived and then try to prepare. We should already be *prepared*.

What can we do to prepare? Well, when there is a threat of a tornado or hurricane, we are told to board up the windows to prevent broken glass and when there is the threats of flooding, people try to place a type of barrier, usually sand bags piled high to change the flow of water or to hold the water back from flooding their property. They also are told to evacuate the place and to go to higher ground.

These are some of the physical things that we can do to prevent the loss of property and life. There are also some things we can do for our spiritual well-being.

The Bible says that in all our ways that we are to acknowledge God so that He can direct our paths. If we want God's strategy for our life we must not forget to acknowledge him and seek his direction in our storms.

What are some of the things we can do to assure our spiritual well-being? We need to get to higher ground in our spiritual life to survive our storms. According to Romans 12:2, we must have a renewed mind so that we may be able to discern what the plan of God is for our life. Whatever his plan, we know that it is good for us and will bring about good results in our situations. God has a perfect will for our life and we should seek him for the things that are acceptable to him; if we faint in the day of adversity; that is unacceptable to the Father.

We need to know what God would have us to do in our storms. What is God's strategy for surviving or weathering our storm? Doing what is not God ordained or should I say doing what is not God's will could cause us to lose family, home, friends, jobs, and our salvation.

GOD'S STRATEGIES

We know from reading the Bible that God takes the foolish things and confounds the wise. David the shepherd boy took five smooth stones and a slingshot and he was able to defeat Goliath. To the wise, of course, it would seem foolish to go up against a man that was over nine feet tall and the point of his spear weighed six hundred shekels, but God's strategy was for a boy to use a slingshot and a stone to overcome and win the battle. This was a foolish thing right?

God's strategy varies from storm to storm, and from man to man, and from problem to problem, so we must acknowledge him so that he can give us his plan for victory or survival.

Jehoshaphat's strategy to win the battle against the Moabites and Ammonites was just to sing and praise God and to give him thanks. So he followed the instruction of God and sent Judah, his choir, out first. God took up his cause and set ambush against the men of Moab and Ammon and Mount Seir. I can hear you now, saying, "This is no time for singing and praising. What I'm dealing with in my life has taken my joy and song." Well, your darkest hour is the right time to sing. The Bible tells us to sing unto the Lord a new song and if you don't have one ask him and he will give you a song so you can go through your storm with joy.

I read that God inhabits the praises of Israel. I don't know about you, but I want God to be where I am when I'm going through. My prayer to God when I'm going through and feeling so very much overwhelmed by the cares of this world is *come dear Savior right down into the midst of whatever trial that I'm going through, rule and reign; your presence is much desired.*

When God is present in our situations, we can be confident that we have access to his wisdom and his knowledge and his strength. We lack the very thing that would cause us to be victorious because we fail to ask for it. Go ahead and ask him now for that song that will carry you through. He is waiting, just ask!

Remember Paul and Silas prayed and sang praises unto God at their midnight hour and they sang so others could hear that even in the prison they still had joy. That is one reason that we should be prepared for the storm so that the circumstances will not take away our joy, because the joy of the Lord is our strength. We may not be happy with the way things are going in our life, but we can still have joy.

God's strategy for you is to *sing*. Sing out loud so that others can hear you praising God in the midst of your storm.

Someone besides God has their eyes on you. What are they seeing and what are they hearing from you in your storm? They are watching your attitude. Are you going through with confidence and faith toward God or are you going through with fear and murmuring and complaining?

God sees you and he has your circumstances all under control. The words that you speak should demonstrate that you are aware that God can handle your situation. Give God the praise in the midst of your storm. Glorify him by the words you speak.

I can hear you singing now, "*Love lifted me; love lifted me, when nothing else could help, love lifted me.*" Wow, you are on your way, all praise be to God!

DON'T FORGET PRAYER

The first thing we should do to prepare is to make sure our prayer life is in good shape. Are you talking to God regularly? When is the last time that you had a little talk with Jesus? Don't be one of those Christians that only talk to God when things are going bad in their life. We should have a consistent prayer life. God should be familiar with our voice and we should be familiar with his. Jesus says, "My sheep know my voice and none other will they follow." Get to know the voice of Jesus Christ through prayer.

Take time to build a relationship with the Father through prayer. Talk to him and give space for him to talk to you. Learn to enjoy his presence in the good times by communing with him so when the bad times come, your heart will not condemn you. You will have confidence that he hears you and you will know that if you ask anything according to his will, you will have the petitions that you desire of him. This confidence comes through relationship building in prayer. How can the Father direct our steps if we never talk to him?

Prayer is an essential key for weathering any storm. Have you heard, little prayer, little power, much prayer, much power. Prayer enables us to endure hardship, pressures, pain, and suffering. Prayer gives us the ability to hold out, to last, to hold up under pressure, and to not faint.

When the adversary comes against your marriage or family, you should go to your knees and fight him with prayer. Many battles are won on our knees. Much insight into our problems is gained on our knees. Prayer is one of the most powerful weapons of warfare that God has given the believer and he expects and wants us to make full use of it. Prayer recharges our spirit man so that he is renewed day by day.

When should we pray? Psalms 55:17 says *"Evening and morning and at noon, will I pray, and cry aloud and he shall hear my voice."*

Why not wake up in the morning and say, "Good morning heavenly Father, King Jesus, Holy Spirit," acknowledging the presence of God right away, giving him his honor and recognition. He's there so speak to him. Give him thanks for a new day and watching over you while you slept. Whatever our situation, we should always find something to be thankful and grateful for. *Tell God thank you.*

You know if we want God to be free to act upon our prayer request, we need to make sure that there is nothing that will prevent him from answering us. Clear the line; remove the static of unforgiveness, resentment, bitterness, and all the things that cause a malfunction on the line.

Why should we pray? The Bible says men ought always pray and not faint and that we are to pray without ceasing. I'm sure that if I hadn't prayed to God and asked him to place forgiveness in my heart for Dave (I will say more about Dave later), I would be a bitter woman today and without joy and God in my life. We pray because God knows what is best for us and we want his solutions to our problems. We pray so that we will not faint. Some things are sent into our life from the adversary and they are meant to cause us to become weak in the knees and to topple over with despair and hopelessness, but a believer that has a consistent prayer life will be able to endure.

Who should you pray for? Pray for yourself that your faith fail not; pray for those that are going through their storms, for Ephesians 6:18 says "Praying always with all prayer and supplication in the Spirit and watching thereunto with all perseverance and supplication for all saints." I'm sure that my mother and the saints of God were praying for me during my stormy season, and because of the peace and joy that I now have in the Lord, I know that their prayers did avail much.

If you allow the Holy Spirit to direct your prayers, you find yourself praying for others that you know that may be going through the same situations as yourself. As a single parent, I was quite familiar with the distresses of trying to run a household on one income and to be mother and father at the same time. Who better can take the troubles of single parent to the Lord than another single parent? Who can better pray with a heart filled with compassion and mercy than one who has experienced the lonely hours with no one to hold you or comfort you after the children have been sung to and tucked away in the bed?

Get your eyes off yourself and look around at those that God brings you in contact with on a daily basis. Do you see their hurt; do you see their pain and sufferings? Intercede for them.

Storms are a trying time and storms come into every believer's life. We need to pray to endure the test of the storm. If we faint in the day of adversity our strength is small. *Prayer makes our strength large!*

Storms of joblessness, rocky marriages and disobedient and rebellious children should drive us to our knees in prayer. They should make us draw neigh unto God. It is only through prayer that we are able to find and abide in that place that God has provided as a refuge; the *Eye of the Storm!*

MY STORM

We didn't have a perfect marriage; we had our ups and downs. I know our situation was a little turbulent at times, but I believed that we would overcome any obstacles and grow old gracefully together. My mother and father were still married and his mother and father were still married, so divorce was not something that I had considered, because at that time, people hung on in there through the bad and through the good. I know many people stayed together for the sake of their children and even thought the fires of love had cooled down to the point where there was barely smoke to indicate that there was ever a burning fire, yet they stayed.

I was prepared to go through and work through whatever, but I was not prepared for the words *"I'm through!"*

Dave had been working at International Harvest, which is a large manufacturer of tractors and other heavy equipment. The company wasn't doing well financially, so they were moving from the Midwest and downsizing. Dave was let go and I must say that he did search diligently to find another job in the area, because he had me and two children to support and a mortgage to pay.

We had a nice home and two nice cars. His and hers, and I give God the praise because he had blessed us at a young age. I got pregnant when I was nineteen and we were married before I turned twenty. We were doing great financially before his layoff, because I had a good job also, working for the phone company, and back in the day that was considered one of the better jobs to have. I was enjoying my lifestyle because we didn't always have things when I was growing up, so I was glad to be married and able to afford the material things.

We were doing fine for awhile; the bills were being paid because I still had my job, but Dave was becoming more irritable because he wasn't working and he was taking care of our daughter instead of putting her in the daycare. We began to argue more and more over small things. Looking back, I guess Dave must have felt insecure because he wasn't providing for his family the way he wanted. He began to go out more at night and to stay later and later, and sometimes he wouldn't return until late the next morning. We would have a big fight and not speak to each other for days, but we would always makeup.

One day, Dave told me that he wanted to go to Atlanta and look for work. He had some relatives there and they would put him up while he searched for work. This was fine with me because I heard that Atlanta was a good place for blacks and I had been there with him on vacation before and I liked what I saw. So we told our families what our intentions were and they offered no objection and gave us their blessings. This would work well for me as far as a job goes, because at that time, Ma Bell was in every state and I was sure that I would be able to transfer my job to whatever city Dave decided to relocate in Georgia.

The day finally arrived for Dave to leave. He packed his little black sports Opal with all that it could hold, which were just a few clothes and his tennis racket. We said our good-byes and he was off.

I went back to work the very next day and told my supervisor that I wanted to put in a transfer to Atlanta and all the surrounding suburbs. He helped me search and to put those transfers in. I told all my co-workers that I would be leaving as soon as my husband found a job. So that became the office gossip, Bess is leaving for Atlanta! I was excited about the move to the big city.

The next thing I had to do was put an ad in the newspaper that I had a house for rent, but I couldn't do that until Dave called to say that he had found a job.

That day came, the long awaited phone call. We couldn't move right away, because he needed to work awhile and to find housing for us. He would come home on some weekends and when he was home, he assured me that our family would be together again just as soon as he could find a place for us. I wasn't happy about the time we had apart, but the reunion each time he came home was just like a honeymoon. I was on cloud nine.

It seemed like forever, but the day finally arrived when Dave called to say that he had found a place and I could go ahead and place that ad in the paper to rent the house and to take any job offers that I might get for Atlanta or Marietta, because these would be close to his job. He said he found a place in the suburb of Marietta, which is outside of Atlanta.

I put the ad in the paper and it didn't take long before I had a renter. The renter was happy to find my house, because it was in a nice neighborhood and I wasn't asking a lot for rent. I gave her my date that I planned to leave, so she gave her landlord the same date. I contracted with a moving company to move our things and I also had a job waiting for me at the Southern Bell in Marietta.

I was beginning to get a little nervous because I had arranged everything and everyone had their dates, the movers, the lady that was renting my house, Southern Bell, and my present employer had the date that I would be leaving my job, but I couldn't get in touch with Dave.

I contacted everyone that I could think of to contact in Atlanta and some of his relatives said they hadn't seen him in weeks. Another said that they gave him my previous messages. My nerves were all shot because he wasn't returning my calls. Have you ever had the gut feeling that someone was going to drop a ton of bricks on you?

I didn't know how they were going to fall or when, but I knew without a shadow of doubt that they were falling.

Finally D-day: Dave called, and after asking him if he was all right, I wanted to know why he hadn't returned my calls. After a long pause, he spoke up and said that he couldn't move us there because the house that he found to rent wasn't as nice as the one that we had and he didn't want to bring us down there to those conditions.

The earth could have opened up and swallowed me right then and I would have welcomed it. I wanted to be anywhere but where I was listening to what I was listening to.

I tried to assure him that everything would work out okay after I got there because I had a job and we would be able to move to another house later on. I told him that I had already rented our house and that the family was expecting to move in next week. I told him that I had the movers and that I had told my boss that I was leaving next week. He told me that he couldn't move us there and that I would have to cancel everything and he hung up.

Beam me up, Scotty; open up planet earth and swallow me, mountains fall on me, but please don't leave me here to face this on my own! I wanted to die! How could he do this to me? What was he thinking? Didn't he care about my feelings in all of this? Sure, leave me here to face these people and to be the brunt of gossip and humiliation; what did he care? I hated him! Yet, I loved him.

I didn't know what to do next. I was confused, dumbfounded, and in total shock and despair. My little world of dreams had just come crumbling down. What would I do now? What would I say to people that would want to know why I wasn't moving? I sat there for what seemed like hours before I moved.

I had this hope that Dave would come to his senses after thinking about the things that I said to him and call back. I kept hearing the sound of the phone ringing and I would walk to the phone and pick it up only to hear the dial tone, because in reality it had not rung, it was only my imagination because this was something that I wanted so badly. I mustered up enough strength to get up and get dressed for bed, but that night must have been the longest night in my life and it seemed like day break would never come.

I tried to contact Dave again the next day, but I wasn't able to reach him. Atlanta is not far from Springfield, and my father said that I could have chosen to go there and check things out for myself, but I didn't. I don't know why I chose not to fly there and see for myself what exactly was going on with my husband, but I didn't. Maybe things would have turned out differently if I had taken the initiative to go there and fight for my man; maybe we would not have gotten a divorce. Who knows but God?

I called forth enough strength and courage to tell my supervisor and my co-workers that I would not be moving after all, and of course, everyone wanted to know why.

I don't recall what I told them, but I'm sure they knew something wasn't right about the situation, especially after I started the divorce proceedings several months later.

I canceled the movers and lost the money that I had put down and I canceled my job transfer and the last thing I did was to tell the lady that was going to rent my house that I would not be leaving.

This was the thing that I remember clearly, because this was the one thing that affected other lives. When I told her that I wouldn't be leaving, she literally begged me to let her rent the house and she pleaded with me not to renege on my promise. She also had three or four children and a husband and now she didn't have anywhere to live because she had given up her place knowing that she was going to have mine.

I was humiliated and embarrassed for myself and her family, but my hands were tied because I had nowhere to go. She cried because I had made a mess of her life. I cried because Dave had made a mess of my life and hers.

I'm not saying that I was all Jesus-centered at that time, because I was not, but one thing I do know: it was only God that strengthened me and gave me courage to carry on my everyday duties as a mother and employee.

The old woman died and a new woman took her place. I was a great pretender, because on the inside I was dying and perhaps one day without me knowing it, I really did die emotionally. I know I had a public face because my co-workers used to say "Girl, you act like nothing has happened and that you wanted a divorce." They just didn't know! I had two children to care for; they needed me and I would be there for them. So any emotions of hurt and pain could only come out after work and after the children were asleep, and then and only then was I free to release *a portion.* I suppressed anger for many years, but it managed to disguise and manifest itself as lateness for everything.

I later discovered that while Dave was job hunting, he became sidetracked by another woman and lost focus on the reason he went to Georgia. Most people would have already come to this conclusion. This is the same story that has been written by many others, just new characters to play it out. The endings will vary, because we can create our own ending.

Dave later married that woman and after one child with her, they got a divorce because she never factored in that Dave would have to pay child support and that his children would come visit and spend the summer and such things.

The storm of abandonment was a tsunami for me, but because of the grace of God, I survived and he has, by his Spirit, healed my wounded spirit and bound up my broken heart. He is restoring my soul day by day through prayer.

NEW BEGINNINGS AFTER THE STORM

Our life dreams may become destroyed or battered, but God will restore all that has been taken or destroyed if you continue to trust and have faith in him. God gives fresh starts and new beginnings, and he certainly is the Lord our God that heals every broken heart and wounded spirit that comes to him. I can testify to that. He truly restores our soul.

Our soul is comprised of our mind and our emotions and our will; God puts it all back in perfect order. He heals the mind and causes it to become a sound mind and now you can think clearly and make right decision. Prayer regulates our emotions, now we can have peace to replace anxiety and nervousness. Prayer causes the will of God to become clear to us. The psalmist said, *"I sought the Lord and he heard me and saved me out of all my troubles."* Knowing his will in our storm brings with it the power and the determination to go through.

I don't know whether I would classify the circumstances of my broken marriage as a tsunami, a flood or a tornado. I just know that the events were very devastating to me and my children. Divorce is a very destructive force to every aspect of the family. One thing I do know is that my world was shaken and rearranged by the events and I had to start all over again with everything fresh and new.

I've had other storms since then, but that first one was *"The Biggie."*

Time has flown by now and I can no longer feel the pain from that storm and I praise God for that, because the pain and the aftershock were at times unbearable. I know firsthand why people say he or she has a broken heart, because there was a time when I actually thought my heart was broken like a plate or cup. Trust me when I tell you I could actually feel the pain physically. Something had happened on the inside of me and I could feel it in my chest area.

We had a blizzard in my hometown, which made everything in my life seem bleak and barren. That was the last straw for me. I knew I had to move, because the weather was symbolic of my life. I needed a fresh start. Looking back over my life I see that God used this blizzard as a catalyst for my new beginning.

I had a brother attending the University of Washington and a friend who was living in Seattle, so I had my brother come drive us across country. My daughter was eight and my son was three at the time of the move. I sold my home, and back in the seventies, I only made a couple thousand as profit. I took a couple of blankets and my encyclopedias and other children's books; packed what clothes we could in my car and off we went. New Beginnings!

> Isaiah 54:4–8: Fear not for thou shalt not be ashamed; neither be thou. Confounded for thou shalt not be put to shame for thou. Shall forget the shame of thy youth, and shalt not remember the reproach of thy widowhood anymore. For thy Maker is thine husband, the Lord of host is his name and thy Redeemer the Holy One of Israel; The God of the whole Earth shall he be called.
>
> For the Lord hath called thee as a woman forsaken and grieved in Spirit, and a wife of youth, when thou was refused, saith thy God. For a small moment have I forsaken thee; but with great mercies will I gather thee. In a little wrath I hid my face from thee for a moment; but with everlasting kindness will I have mercy on thee, saith the Lord thy Redeemer.

My marriage was not able to weather that storm of life, but my soul was saved. God saw to it that I came out with life, eternal life. Praise be to God! Storms can drive us to the safety of God. God has been my greatest comforter and shelter in the many storms that I have gone through. I have his assurance that if he did it once, he will do it again. All I need to do is cast all of my cares on Him through prayer. There is a song that says it all for me. Let me share it:

> Sweet hour of prayer! Sweet hour of prayer! That calls me from a world of care, and bids me at my Father's throne, make all my wants and wishes known. In seasons of distress and grief my soul has often found relief, and oft escaped the tempter's snare, by thy return, sweet hour of prayer. Amen

I knew I had to forgive Dave for deserting me and the children, and I prayed to God asking him to place forgiveness in my heart. I'm sure he heard me when I first asked, and the Holy Spirit went to work, but the damage to my heart was so extensive that I didn't see the result of the work of the Lord immediately. Healing for me was a process. The more I prayed and stayed in the presence of God and his people the more care he was able to give me so that healing could be complete.

I don't know where I would be if I had not learned to pray. I have received much strength and comfort through communing with the Heavenly Father on a daily basis. He has revealed himself to me as a Father and as a friend. Actually, I have found him to be exactly what I've needed in every given situation. It is truly a mystery how God can meet all of our needs. Christ the mystery.

Now that we have seen how vital prayer is to the believer; let's move to the next thing the believer should do to survive his storm.

OTHER ACTIONS DRESS FOR SUCCESS

Secondly, *put ye on the Lord Jesus Christ.* We must have on Christ in order to weather any storm. Ephesians 4:24 says, *"And that ye put on the new man, which after God is created in righteousness and true holiness."* I like this because in putting on the new man, which is Christ; we will have to put off the old man with his deeds. The deeds of the old man are the very things that would hinder us or cause us not to come through victoriously.

Put on the right clothes! We most definitely want to make sure that we are wearing the right clothes. If is raining cats and dogs and thundering ferociously, wear your rain gear and when it is freezing and there is snow and ice on the ground where your snow shoes and warm coat and gloves and hat. It is important to be properly dressed for the storm.

I'm mindful of a news report I heard a couple days ago. We had a snow storm in the area and a man and his family were caught in the storm. As they were driving from Seattle to Oregon, they ran out of gas and after a day of being stranded, the man decided to leave his family and go for help. When the search and rescue team went out to find them, they found his family alive, but the husband was not found until a couple days later far from his family. He had not survived because he was not properly dressed when he ventured out into that storm. Ephesians 6:10–18 says:

> Finally, my brethren, be strong in the Lord, and in the Power of his might. Put on the whole armour of God, that ye may be able to stand against the wiles of the devil. For we wrestle not against flesh and blood, but against principalities, against powers, against the rulers of the darkness of this world, against spiritual wickedness in high places. Wherefore take unto you the whole armour of God, that Ye may be able to withstand in the evil day, and having done all to stand.

It is very important to make sure that we have on our life jacket when the waters are raging. It is essential to put ye on the Lord Jesus Christ, who is our life jacket, being strong in the Lord and in the power of his might and we are ready for our storm. Paul goes on to name the pieces of the armor, salvation, the breastplate of righteousness, and truth, and the Word of God and faith, and we don't want to forget to pray. When we have put all these things on; we are properly dressed; then we are prepared to weather the storm.

We need to make sure that we have God on our side, because if God be for us, who can be against us? Make sure that you are saved. Have you accepted Christ Jesus as your personal savior? If so, then you can put him on. If not, then you can still put him on right now!

Repeat after me: *Lord Jesus, I am a sinner; come into my life now and save me from my sins. Wash me with your blood and fill me with your spirit. I repent of my sins so come into my heart and be lord of my life right now. I thank you God for your son and for saving me right now, in Jesus name, Amen and Amen.*

Great, now you are Christ's and he is now watching over you. Praise God and welcome to the household of faith. Now you have the covering of God's Spirit. Okay, now that you are a child of God, go ahead get dressed.

Gird yourself with the Word of God, which is truth, and then you will be able to stand when the onslaughts or attacks of the devil rise in your life to shake you from your position with God. Satan is the author and the father of lies, so he will try to deceive you anyway he can to make you think that God will not protect you or bring you through your storms. He is a lie. God loves you and he is there for you whenever you call night or day.

Make sure you have covered your chest area with righteous living. Cover your heart. The Bible says that we are to guard our hearts with all diligence for out of it flows the issues of life. I just believe that out of our heart will come the problems (issues) that we deal with on a daily basis, whether on our jobs, in our families, at our churches, all these areas of our life will reflect the chest condition. We must make sure that the chest or heart area is covered by the breastplate of righteousness.

I can recall there was a period in my life when I was being disobedient to my pastor. I noticed after awhile is that same condition began to show up in my home as disobedient children and in my work place with disobedient employees. God was trying to get my attention to let me know that I was the cause of this storm or turmoil in my life, and all I needed to do to bring peace again in all areas was to change my behavior toward my pastor. I had to change my heart condition.

PASS THE TEST

Did you ever think that maybe the storms that arrive in our life come to reveal to us just what we are made of and on what we have built our life and hope? Jesus described two men, one was wise and the other was foolish. "And the rain descended, and the floods came, and the winds blew, and beat upon the house, and it fell not, for it was founded upon a rock." Jesus also said, "And the rain descended, and the floods came, and the winds blew, and beat upon the house and it fell and great was the fall of it because it was built upon the sand." The latter man was foolish because he built upon the sand.

What are you building your life hopes and dreams upon: the rock or the sand? Not only will our foundation be tested, but our character as well. The strength of a man will show up in the storm and also his weakness.

We must remember as the song writer says, "Our hope is built on nothing less than Jesus and his righteousness. I dare not trust the sweetest frame but wholly lean on Jesus name, on Christ the solid rock I stand. All other ground is sinking sand." I'm not saying this is the easiest thing to do but I have learned, and I'm still learning, to trust God even in everything.

Like I said, I believe the storms are sent to test us. I hear you asking, "Test what"? Well, your faithfulness for one thing; and then there is your stability, your humility, your backbone, your strength; will you go through or do you tuck your tail and run.

Your mouth is another thing that will be tested. I heard you, "My mouth?" Yes, your mouth! Are you all talk and no action? Does your talk match your walk?

There is a saying that says "When the going gets tough, the tough get going." This means they roll up their sleeves and get to work. This means that they will not run when things get hard. God already knows just what is in us, but he wants us to know for ourselves how far we have come on this Christian journey.

Peter thought that he was ready to die for Jesus, but when the test of loyalty came, he denied ever knowing him. Now Jesus knew that was in Peter all along, but Peter's lack of courage, loyalty, and strength had to be revealed to Peter himself. He was not ready yet. He was not tough yet.

When the test comes, God wants you to remember that it is only a test and you will need to pass or repeat. Just how tough are you? Can you stand the test? Can you pass?

The Bible says, 1 Peter 4:12–13,

Beloved think it not strange concerning the fiery trial which is to try you, as though some strange thing happened unto you. But rejoice, inasmuch as ye are partakers of Christ's sufferings; that, when his glory shall be revealed ye may be glad also with exceeding joy.

We need to arm ourselves with the same mind that Christ had. Think about it; Daniel was tested when he was thrown into the lion's den, and the Hebrew boys were tested when they were thrown into the fiery furnace, and Job was tested when he was turned over to Satan, and Joseph was tested when he was thrown into the pit and sold to slaves. Our Lord and Savior was tested when he was led into the wilderness by the Spirit and when he was in the Garden of Gethsemane. *You will be tested! Get ready! Prepare!*

The Bible says, "Wherefore seeing we also are compassed about with so great a cloud of witnesses, let us lay aside every weight and the sin which doth so easily beset us, and let us run with patience the race that is set before. Looking unto Jesus the author and finisher of our faith who for the joy that was set before him endured the cross, despising the shame, and is set down at the right hand of the throne of God."

My brethren, count it all joy when ye fall into divers temptations: Knowing this, that

the trying of your faith worketh patience. But
let patience have her perfect work, that ye may
be perfect and entire, wanting nothing.
James 1:1–4.

Storms are sent to work something out of us, or to work something into us. Remember, God is the one that is doing the working by his Holy Spirit, and if you will work with him, you will pass the test with flying colors.

Storms are sent to mature us, to give us spiritual muscles, and to establish us in the faith. Storms can also be sent to chasten us so we will learn to obey. What is your storm trying to test you on today? Is your faith being tested, or perhaps it is your trust level that needs to have an overhaul? How are you faring in your obedience to God? Is your love for God and for mankind a little on the shaky side? Are you a persistent person or are you easily persuaded to give up? Is your character being tested? Has your integrity been weighed and found to be lacking? Whatever the test, you will discover that his grace truly is sufficient for you. *Go through!*

Let's take a look at a few people and see just how they handled their storm and notice whether they survived or not. Were they prepared? I hope after you read my examples, that you will ready yourself for your storm.

JOHN AND MARY'S STORM TEST

John and Mary were the ideal couple to all who saw them together; they seemed to be perfectly matched in looks and personality. Their marriage seemed to be made in heaven. I mean, they had the house with the two-car garage, and two children that were quite cute, loving, and obedient to their parents; no teenage woes there.

John was a deacon in the church and Mary was a committed choir member who had the ability to sing those solos telling of the goodness of God under the anointing and power of God. A godly example of a couple committed to God and each other.

John was branch manager for one of the leading banks in town and he was expecting to receive a raise on the day the boss called him into the office; but to his surprise, the boss told him that the bank was being sold to one of their competitors and that his position was being eliminated because the new owners wanted to downsize by cutting the job of one manager and a couple of tellers.

"Oh no, not now Lord, this is not the time to bring this sort of change into my life. Mary just told me last night that we were expecting to have a new baby by summer. Wow, Lord, what a shocker, now what? I was hoping to go places with this bank."

"John, John, are you listening?" His boss was staring at him as though he was waiting for a response to a question. "John, we appreciate your loyalty and all your hard work, but we must cut back to remain competitive."

John could feel his emotions changing from disappointment to anger, and before he knew it, he just exploded. "What about me, huh? What about me? I have a family to take care of and a new baby on the way. I have a mortgage that has to be paid, now what am I going to do? I have busted my buns for this bank for the last ten years and this is the thanks I get? Well, forget you too."

"Calm down, John," his boss said. "We will give you a good severance and an excellent recommendation, because you were truly an asset to this bank."

"Sure," John said, as he stormed out of his boss's office and slammed the door.

John jumped in his car and drove home to tell Mary the bad news. When he opened the door, he could tell that she wasn't in a good mood. "Hi babe," she said. "Dinner is running a little late tonight because I am not feeling that great today. I left work early because of pregnancy reasons. How did your day go? I hope it was better than mine. You'll have to go to prayer by yourself tonight, I'm not up to it."

"Mary, come sit down, I have something to tell you."

As she approached him, she must have noticed the look on his face, so she stopped in her tracks and said, "Is this bad news? I don't feel like hearing anything negative today; can it wait?"

"No," he said. "Come and sit down." She sat down in the nearest chair and threw her head back and closed her eyes.

"I was let go today. The bank was sold to one of our competitors and they let me go to cut cost."

"Don't worry babe," she said. "God will supply our needs. He will provide you with another job. I know you must be thinking this is not the time for this because of my pregnancy, but we will be okay." She moved from the chair to the couch, where I was sitting, and put her arms around me. "John, you know the word, when two touch and agree, they have what they ask, so take this request to the prayer group tonight, and you watch, God will answer."

John was not able to find another job as quickly as he thought and he was getting bored with having to take on the responsibility of making sure the dinner was ready and the house cleaned by the time his wife arrived home. It seemed to him that Mary was taking advantage of her pregnancy and his unemployed state. Not only that, but their bank account was being depleted and they were down to their last thousand. Jeff, their sixteen-year-old, was acting out by skipping school some days, and John found out after searching his bedroom one day that he was smoking marijuana.

These pressures began to wear John down, and one day, when shopping for groceries, he decided why not by a six-pack of beer just to take the edge off. It's not like he was an alcoholic or something, and he would just drink one bottle a day so he wouldn't get drunk. *I believe the sin is when you get drunk,* he thought to himself. *I'm not hurting anyone and there is no harm done. Right?*

So that day, John believed Satan's lie and opened the door and he came in to rest for awhile. John found that he had to buy beer every time he went grocery shopping and then he began to add wine, and from wine to hard liquor. John had stopped attending church and prayer meetings, and began to frequent one of the bars in town.

Mary contacted her pastor and told him why she and John were not attending church on a regular basis anymore. She couldn't come because as her date of delivery came closer, she found she was too tired to press her way out to church. She told the pastor that her marriage was rocky since John lost his job and the children were getting out of hand. They were rebellious and running with the wrong crowd at school. She wanted to come in for counseling to try and salvage her marriage and family, because she believed that with some help, things could turn around and they could rise above this. The pastor agreed to meet with her and John to give them some tools to overcome the turbulence in their life.

Mary went home from work and told John that she would like to go to counseling with the pastor, but he said "no." He didn't need counseling because he knew what he was doing and, as a matter-of-fact, he wanted a divorce because he had found someone that would not be nagging him every time he turned around about God and church.

"Where is God when you need him? Huh? Where is God when it comes time to pay these bills that are stacking up from month to month? I found a job today without God's help and after the baby is born, I'm leaving."

Mary said, "John, God never left you, but you left him; he has always been there and regardless of what you might, think he did provide that job for you."

"Sure," John said, as he grabbed his coat and his hat and walked out of the house leaving Mary in tears.

He got in his car and drove toward the local bar, but before he could reach the bar, the Spirit of God spoke to him and told him to stop and to go back home where he belonged. God began to speak to his heart and convicted him of the sins he had committed against him, and the pain and hurt he has caused his wife and children.

He pulled over the car and began to sob and confess his sins and to ask the Lord to forgive his sins. After John's encounter with the Holy Spirit the peace of God began to flood his very soul and a great calm came over him. He took out his cell phone and dialed his pastor and told him that he wanted to come in for counseling. John started the car and returned home to find his wife waiting for him with an open heart.

What a mighty God we serve he can take our impossible situations and turn them to possible and can cause our bitter things to become sweet, but we must trust him and never doubt his ability, his power, and his love for us.

This financial storm was sent to test the stability of John and Mary's foundation. There are many couples who crumble under the pressures of a financial crisis when these winds of testing blow. They can be saved or unsaved; it doesn't matter. They can be married for thirty years or five years; many marital foundations will crumble when tried by a financial storm.

Instead of remaining a unit, John and Mary drifted apart and became separate. Instead of clinging to each other for emotional support and strength, a rift took place in the relationship and where they used to be one; they became two.

John and Mary had an advantage in this storm, because they were not alone; they had each other. As Proverbs 4:12 says, "Two are better than one; because they have a good reward for their labor. For if they fall; the one will lift up his fellow; but woe to him that is alone when he falls; for he has not another to help him up." Again, if two lie together, then they have heat but how can one be warm alone? And if one prevails against him two shall withstand him and a threefold cord is not quickly broken.

We are not too faint, but to be strong and courageous in any given situation because we are not alone. God is with us and not only is he with us but he is for us and we know that he sees our need and that he will provide. We must trust God and stay focused and wait on him.

John and Mary's marriage and family life was restored and now they are able to tell others that God is a provider and that he will come through for you just like his Word says he will. They have also been made stronger in this storm. God has given them a testimony for other couples that may be going through similar circumstances. Psalm ninety-one says, "He that dwells in the secret place of the most High shall abide under the shadow of the Almighty." When we stay in the presence of God; we have his provisions for life.

JANICE'S STORM TEST

Let's take a look at another witness of God's grace and goodness.

Janice was a woman full of energy, life, and vitality; there was no stopping her. "Miss Busyness," she was always on the move. She was single and she loved the Lord, so she intended to keep herself busy in the work of the Lord until he sent Mister Right into her life. Miss Energetic was not going to let the grass grow under her feet; she had places to go, people to meet, and things to do it seemed every night of the week. We all loved Janice, just being in her presence made you feel alive. She was such a sweet person and full of the Holy Ghost. She had a love for people and not just the people of God. Janice was truly an ambassador for Christ.

Janice had been feeling a little tired lately and she couldn't seem to pull herself out of it, so she scheduled a doctor's appointment just to make sure that she hadn't caught some type of virus or bacteria. She had been on a mission trip to India for about four weeks and since she got back, she hadn't been feeling up to par. She tried to be very careful about what she ate and drank there, but something must have happened because she can't shake this nausea that happened every now and then. She found that her energy level was not what it used to be.

"What is going on doctor?" she asked. "What are the results of all those tests that you ran on me last week"? The doctor didn't look up from her chart immediately, but she could tell that he was looking for the right words for her.

"Janice, it's not good. I'm afraid that your problem is more serious than I thought. You have cancer and it is quite progressive. We can operate to see just how far it has spread throughout your body, but it doesn't look good. You should start putting your house in order."

"What do you mean doctor," she asked?

He replied, "The cancer is terminal."

Janice could not believe her ears, what was going on here? *I eat right and I belong to a gym and exercise almost every day. I take good care of myself because I wanted to make sure that this type of thing would not come my way. This is not fair. I'm only thirty years old and there are many things that I want to do in life. God where are you and how could you let this happen to me? What did I do to deserve this? God are you listening; what is going on here?*

Her thoughts were racing through her mind so fast that she could not keep up with them and her silent conversation with God was interrupted by the doctor when he asked, "Is it okay to set the surgery up for next Tuesday"?

"Sure," she said. "Whatever you say is fine with me."

"Janice, are you going to be all right to drive home alone?" asked, the doctor.

"Sure," she said. "I need the time alone; I'll be fine."

Janice doesn't remember how she got home that day, but God must have sent his angels to go before her to make sure that there were no accidents, because she certainly doesn't remember driving herself home or turning the key in the door and entering her apartment.

She turned the ringer on her phones off because she didn't want the silence broken; what she needed now was perfect peace and quiet. It was high noon, but she took her clothes off, closed all blinds, and got into the bed and pulled the covers over her head and had a good cry. "God are you there?" she asked. Nothing but silence. "God are you there?" she asked again. More silence.

Storms can arrive suddenly and catch us unprepared to cope or catch us fully armed and ready for battle. This was the time in Janice's life that she was caught prepared for whatever trial would come her way. Now how was she prepared?

She had been developing her relationship with God the Father in a consistent manner by talking to him on a daily basis. They call this being prayed up. She didn't want to have the type of relationship with God where she only called upon him in the time of trouble, so she learned early in her Christian walk to wake up with her mind stayed on the Lord. She would rise early and seek him just like the Word says, and have a time of praise and worship and prayer before she left the house, thanking God for his goodness toward her and for his presence in her life.

She was also consistent in reading the Word and meditating in his Word. She was not as consistent in her fasting as she wanted to be, but she tried to offer to the Lord at least once or twice a week.

Janice contacted her spiritual father and mother in Atlanta and advised them of her condition and asked them to stand in agreement with her for a divine healing. God had given her a Word that he was going to heal her. She would live and not die. Janice had made up in her heart and mind that she was going to believe the report of the Lord instead of the doctor's. Her pastor and the entire church family went on a three-day consecration for her by only drinking water and juice for three days. After this time, the Word came forth that she would live and not die.

Janice was encouraged by the Word that came to her about her healing, but in the coming weeks, the cancer began to try her faith. Was she going to hold onto God's promise to heal her, or was she going to listen to the voice of doubt and unbelief from friends and foes?

As she began to suffer with pain, weight loss, lack of energy and vitality; this had a great negative effect on her spirit and she found herself slipping into a state of depression. She was accustomed to much movement, but now she was becoming a prisoner of this disease.

Instead of her running here and there helping others, she now needed much help and comfort herself. Janice discovered something about herself, and that was that she liked being the one giving and doing, but she was not comfortable on the receiving end. She ministered much kindness and love and comfort to others, so the Father was faithful in repaying it back to her and her cup ran over.

Janice laid in bed thinking of Jesus in the Garden of Gethsemane as he prayed unto the Father asking him, "If it be possible, let this cup pass from me, nevertheless not as I will but as thy will." She also wanted to be relieved of the cup that had been given to her to drink from, but like our Lord, she knew she must submit and say, "Nevertheless, not my will, but thy will be done." She thought of how Jesus had great agony to remain in the will of God and to glorify him by giving his life for her and all mankind. The Holy Spirit comforted her with this song.

> When peace like a river attended my way
> When sorrows like a sea billow roll
> Whatever my plight thou has taught me to say
> It is well; it is well with my soul

Though satan should buffet, though trials
may come
Let this blessed assurance control
That Christ has regarded my helpless estate
And has shed his own blood for my soul
It is well; it is well with my soul

When the Holy Spirit finished ministering to her by
this song, she had such peace flowing through her that it
was scary, but she knew that she would be able to endure
to the end and was going through this illness with the
Father by her side; she could rest now with the assurance
that she was not alone in this storm. What peace and
security this brought to her. She was not forgotten!

Janice had become extremely sick. The cancer had
stripped her of her strength, and she was admitted to the
hospital for treatment. The doctors were still not giving
her any hope; even though she told them that God had
assured her that he would heal her. One doctor did confess to her that he believed in the power of prayer and
medicine mixed together and had seen the positive results of the mixture. He encouraged her in her faith, but
she could tell he was not convinced that God could turn
her situation around.

Janice was awakened early one morning while in the
hospital by birds chirping outside her window. One bird
was actually on the window sill looking in at her and it
sounded like he was singing especially to her. It was such
a beautiful morning and the light of a new day flooded

her room. The bird continued to sit and stare and sing. What peace and joy filled her heart at that moment, and she felt the presence of the Lord all over her. Her body was filled with a warm sensation from head to toe, and she knew it was the Lord healing her of cancer.

As she listened to the bird sing, she thought of her favorite song, "His Eye is on the Sparrow," and this gave her much comfort. The half cannot be told of the love and joy and peace she had at that moment filling her very being. She knew within herself that a change had taken place. She had heard other people's testimonies, but now she had her own testimony of the grace of God that heals. There was such lightness in her body she had to reach down and feel if she was still laying there. The light that filled the room wasn't just from the sun, but it was the glory of God illuminating that hospital room as well as her heart.

She heard a small voice say, "Rest, for you will be leaving this place soon. Rest now, my beloved." She must have dozed off, because when she awoke again, the nurse was in her room changing the intravenous bottle and asking her how she was feeling this morning. Janice said she was feeling great and asked if she could go home soon. The nurse replied that her doctor would be coming in later this afternoon and she could ask him then, but her vital signs were looking very good.

She told the doctor of her earlier experience that morning and asked him if he would run some tests to see if her cancer was still there. She could tell that he didn't want to do this, but she insisted. They ran more x-rays and a few tests just to appease her, but she was confident that they would not find the cancer.

The next day, the doctor came to her room with the x-rays and said that something had happened, because there is no trace of cancer in her body. They wanted to do the x-ray again, because they were dealing with a terminal illness and they wanted to remove the margin of error. The result was the same the second time: no cancer. The doctors were amazed and told her, "Well, we guess you got your miracle."

The Bible says who has believed our report? And to whom is the arm of the Lord revealed?

God will take us safely through our storms, but we must believe that he is able so he can reveal his strength and power to us. We must maintain our confidence, not in our self, but in God's faithfulness and in his love for us.

The Bible also says, "Cast not away therefore your confidence, which has great recompense of reward. For ye have need of patience that, after ye have done the will of God, ye might receive the promise." 1 John 5:14–15 says, "And this is the confidence that we have in him that, if we ask any thing according to his will, he heareth us. And if we know that he hear us, whatsoever we ask, we know that we have the petitions that we desired of him."

Janice had received from God a promise of healing, so she had a right to confidently say, "I shall live and not die," and to wait patiently for the manifestation of her healing. Phillippians 1:6 "Being confident of this very thing that he which hath begun a good work in you will perform it until the day of Jesus Christ.

God will not forget you. He will make his promise good. We just need to learn to wait on him.

Janice came through her storm and discovered that she truly had built her house on the solid rock of Christ Jesus. If she remembers what God did for her in her time of sickness, she will be equipped to weather the next storm. If she abides in the eye of the storm, she will be safe in the Master's arms. This storm of sickness arose suddenly in Janice's life and just as suddenly her healing came.

Janice was determined to hold fast to God's promise to heal her, so therefore, she received her healing. I thought of Jacob as he wrestled with God for his blessing; I thought of Job who said, "Though he slay me yet, will I trust in him, But I will maintain mine own ways before him and he also will be my salvation."

Our heavenly Father is a God of integrity; if he said it he shall perform it. For the Word of God says, "God is not a man that he should lie; neither the son of man that he should repent; has he said, and shall he not do it; or has he spoken, and shall he not make it good?" Being determined and having confidence in God will cause you to stay put and wait on the Lord.

SURVIVAL KEYS

The was nothing unique about my marital problems nor about John and Mary's financial woes or Janice's bout with cancer; these were simply examples of the kinds of situations that will arrive in anyone's life to shake us up and move us to the next place on life's journey. These unpleasant natural occurrences can either make us or break us.

Can you trust God to handle your problem? If not, then you need to stop singing that song asking the Spirit of the living God fall afresh on me and mold me, break me, shape me, and make me, because those are just words that you don't mean. Storms mold us and they help shape and make us into the person that God desires us to be. We must trust God to bring us out all right.

There are some survival keys that will bring you through any storm life will bring your way with your faith toward God intact. Our relationship with the heavenly Father is our most valuable possession and if it can be stolen away from us by adverse circumstances of life then the enemy will have won a great battle and gained our most valued treasure.

Now let's look at a few keys to weathering our storms and if we master these then through it all we shall come through victoriously.

I am mindful of the time the disciples and Jesus were in a ship and there arose a great storm of wind, and the wave beat into the ship, so that it was full of water. The disciples lost focus and began to look at the power of the wind instead of the power of Christ. They forgot that Jesus cared about them, for they cried out, "Master, carest thou not that we perish"? (Mark 4:38). They forgot not only that Jesus cares, but that he was there with them in the storm, only he had peace, because he knew the power of his Father to save.

Our heavenly Father does care whether we perish or prosper. He wants us to succeed in all we do, but he also cares about our spiritual growth. He also wants us to be buff in the spirit. So he allows challenges to strengthen our spiritual muscles. He promised not to put more on us than we can bear and he won't.

The disciples cried unto Jesus and he arose and rebuked the wind and said unto the sea "Peace, be still," (Mark 4:39) and the wind ceased and there was a great calm. I'm sure John and Mary were feeling overwhelmed as the bills began to pile up and their creditors began to call over and over requesting payments; I'm sure they felt like those disciples. "Master do you care that we are going down? Look at us, we are drowning here."

John lost focus and began to seek refuge outside of God. He turned to alcohol and another woman to find comfort and strength. He forgot the promise of God to neither leave nor forsake us. Mary began to feel distant from God because of the cares of her marriage and children. She lost interest in reading the Word and praying. God wants us to turn to him when trouble comes and he will help us to overcome. It is not easy to stay focused, but we must, in order to weather our storms.

When I say stay focused, I mean stay focused on God. Look at him. Look at his faithfulness; focus on his exceeding great and precious promises instead of your problems. Look at his greatness and his mercy, his sovereignty. See him as bigger than any problem that you can ever face. Get a visual; use your healthy imagination. See God in your mind's eye as a mighty dragon slayer and your problems are the dragon. Now see God take out his magnificent sword and slay him. Wow, what a mighty God we serve! What power is in his Word!

Satan will send all kinds of distractions to cause you to become problem focused instead of God focused. Now distractions can take on many forms. One example that comes to mind is you are already experiencing financial hardship and now you are facing a major illness with no medical insurance, and why does your teenager that has been problem free decide one day at the mall to shoplift? These are distractions! They are sent to pull your eyes off God. *Stay focused!*

SURVIVING BY FAITH

We know that we need faith to survive our storms, but fear will come to crush it out. Faith and fear cannot exist at the same time; you will either have one or the other.

After Jesus rebuked the wind, he asked the disciples, "*Why are you so fearful? How is it that you have no faith?*" I believe that fear will come to overtake us, but we should not succumb to it. When things beyond our control happen to us, we should just stop and take a deep breath. Get centered in Christ and then ask ourself, "What am I afraid of? Why am I fainting?"

So the question is still appropriate, "Why are you so fearful?" In the disciples' case, I believe that they were afraid of dying because they asked, "Jesus careth not that we perish?" Remember John and Mary? Well in John's case, I believe that he may have feared losing his house that he had worked so hard to attain, and his manhood, because he could not provide for his family the way he desired, after all, he had become the house husband while his wife worked. It didn't help matters that he felt rejected because he didn't get job offers after interviewing. So he had to deal with the fear of failure. Nevertheless, God has not given us the spirit of fear, but of power, love, and a sound mind.

Fear begins to take root in our life when we lose sight of the power of God or to attribute more power to ourselves or our circumstances. It is by him that we live and move and have our being. We have to trust God with our most valued possessions and the people that we love. In the book of Isaiah 41:10 God says, "Fear thou not for I am with thee be not dismayed for I am they God; I will strengthen thee; yea I will help thee; yea, I will uphold thee with the right hand of my righteousness." When we begin to feel fearful this is the time to call on the name of Jesus to cast out all doubt and to ask him to intercede for us that our faith fail not.

We must believe that he is able to keep that which we have committed to him. The day of the storm, the day of evil, the day of grief, the day of abandonment; the day of sickness and disease however the storm presents itself we must remember to do as Jesus told the disciples *Have faith in God!*

Jesus also asked those same disciples the question, "Where is your faith?" We can be assured of this very thing that the fear factor will arise in our storms, but we must conquer it to have victory in any given situation. In order to be victorious and more than a conqueror, we must live and walk by faith and not by what we are experiencing emotionally or seeing with our eyes.

We can become so emotionally charged by the affects of the storm that we fail to remember Jesus is on our boat and he is sleeping peacefully. We also can have that same peace that he had. We can wake him up by calling his name. Remember, all that call on the name of Jesus shall be saved.

God requires that we have faith in him. He gave it to us and he wants us to use it in the times of trouble. I don't know about you, but it pleases me when my children seek me out for Godly counsel and directions when they encounter a problem or some situation that has them stumped. I'm pleased, because it gives me joy to know they have confidence in me and my guidance. Well, we please our Heavenly Father when we have faith toward him. We also please him when we seek him out by reading his Word and prayer.

When we take our problems to God, we are acknowledging him as God and we are also letting him know that we know that he has exactly what we need. We are stating by our faith in him that he has the solution to our problem. We keep our faith in operation when we focus on God's greatness and not on how large our problem seems to be.

One way to make sure we don't lose faith is to meditate in the Word night and day until our spirit man has developed enough power to overcome the fear factor. The

Bible says we are to build ourselves up in our most holy faith, praying in the Holy Ghost.

Our faith is on trial in every storm. Jesus told Peter, (Luke 22:31) "Simon behold, satan hath desired to sift you as wheat. But I have prayed for thee that thy faith fail not." Our Lord would not have told him that if our faith could not fail.

Remember, Peter would have walked on the water when he got out of the boat if he had kept his eyes on Jesus and not on the fierce winds. Jesus rebuked him by saying, "O ye of little faith." Our faith can fail and it can be little! I have tried at various times in my life to get out of the boat and walk on water, but I didn't have enough faith to sustain the walk.

I remember once when I wanted to leave the familiar territory of working for the phone company and to try my hand at something else. I left my job at AT&T for twenty-five years. I received a nice severance, but when I didn't find another job right away and one that paid the nice salary that I was used to getting, I soon lost faith and ran right back to the familiar job that I was tired of doing.

1 Peter 1:5–9 says that the trial of your faith being much more precious than of gold that perish, though it be tried with the fire might be found unto praise and honor and glory at the appearing of Jesus Christ.

Now the chain of events that took place in Job's life would not represent the average thunder storm, but would be classified as a whirlwind experience or a hurricane; this storm created destruction and damage in his life. Now the whirlwind was not from God to teach him to be obedient or to get his attention, but it was a storm that God allowed to come his way to show the devil just what stuff was in Job's character and how much Job loved the Lord.

> Job 1:8–12: And the Lord said unto Satan, hast thou considered my servant Job, that there is none like him in the earth, a perfect and an upright man, one that feareth God and escheweth evil? Then satan answered the Lord, and said, doth Job fear God for nought? Hast not thou made an hedge about him, and about his house, and about all that he hath on every side? Thou hast blessed the work of His hands and his substance is increased in the land. But put forth thine hand now and touch all that he hath and he will curse thee to thy face. And the Lord said unto Satan, behold, all that he hath is in Thy power, only upon himself put not forth thine hand. So Satan went forth from the presence of the Lord.

God didn't send this storm, but he allowed this whirlwind to infiltrate Job's life. This became a spiritual battle for Job. God didn't intervene, Job had to duke it out with the devil to maintain his integrity and fear of God. Job lost all his worldly goods and family except his wife, who at one point was a thorn in his side. His health deteriorated to the point that his wife told him to curse God and die. Yet through it all, Job held on to his integrity. Job 13:15, "Though he slay me, yet will I trust him…" the NIV says. "Though he slay me yet will I hope in him…" Job knew that if he had committed sins that God would forgive him and he trusted God to bring him through this situation all right.

Some situations that happen in our life are there to help us know just who God is and what he can do. Job 42:5 says, "I have heard of thee by the hearing of the ear, but now mine eye seeth thee." A lot of people have heard of Jehovah-jireh, but few have met the God that provides for them.

We have heard that he will restore all that the cankerworm has eaten, but to see and experience this for ourselves makes God so very real to us. Many things will happen to us in our lifetime, and we will seek God for the reasons why and receive no answer.

We will do a lot of looking back over our life trying to find the sin that brought this thing upon us, but finding nothing; we will cry out, "Why God"? And still receive no explanation, because you see, God owes us no explanation.

When we don't understand why life has dealt us such a hard hand to play, we must continue to hope and trust and have faith toward God. Job's faith went under tremendous testing, but it survived the onslaughts of the devil and he was rewarded for his faithfulness. *He was restored all!*

CHOOSING TO TRUST

Just like the child trusts his dad to catch him when he is told by him to jump from the stairs into his arms; so it is with God. We must have child like faith and trust our heavenly Father to catch us when the wind of the storm is tossing us every which way but loose. We must trust that when we do begin to land, it will be safely in his arms.

Trusting God means to believe that he will and can handle your situation and like Jeremiah 29:22–12 says, "For I Know the thoughts that I think toward you, saith the Lord, thoughts of peace, and not of evil, to give you an expected end. Then shall ye call upon me, and ye shall go and pray unto me, and I will hearken unto you." This great hymn says it all.

Tis so sweet to trust in Jesus, Just to take Him at his word
Just to rest upon his promise; just to
know, thus saith the Lord
Jesus, Jesus, how I trust Him! How
I've proved him o'er and o'er

Jesus, Jesus, precious Jesus! O for grace to trust him more!
I'm so glad I learned to trust Thee, pre-
cious Jesus, Savior, friend
And I know that thou art with me,
will be with me to the end.
Jesus, Jesus, how I trust Him! How
I've proved Him o'er and o'er!
Jesus, Jesus, precious Jesus! O for grace to trust Him more!

When we truly learn to trust God, we will find that we are able to do as our Lord was doing when he was on that boat with the disciples during the storm. *Sleep!* We will sleep, because we are trusting that God will take care of us and handle our situation. It will be that childlike faith and trust.

When we do rise up, we will do as Jesus did and speak to our circumstances. *Peace be still!* One of my favorite Scriptures is Isaiah 32:17–18, which states, "and the work of righteousness shall be peace; and the effect of righteousness quietness and assurance forever." "And my people shall dwell in a peaceable habitation, and in sure dwellings and in quiet resting places."

The reason I like this Scripture is because it keeps me in check. When I begin to think in unrighteous ways, this word becomes spirit and life and can cause my thinking to come in line with what God's Word says. I found out that only righteous thinking will produce quietness and assurance.

Right thinking will cause you to have quietness in your spirit so you can wait on God to bring a change to the turbulence in your life. There will be stillness and calmness and you will have a peace in your spirit knowing that God is working in your behalf and there will be a *divine knowing* that everything is going to be all right.

Now we know that if righteous thinking produces quietness and assurance, then unrighteous thinking will produce unrest, worry, anxiety, doubt, and unbelief and every other negative thing to cause our storm to rage inwardly as well as outwardly; but if we want to have that perfect peace that comes from abiding in the eye of the storm, then we need to make sure that we are renewing our mind on a daily basis in the Word of God.

The Bible says that God will keep in perfect peace all whose minds are stayed on him. This is the key: keeping our minds on God and not on our circumstances. When we do this, we will be rewarded with the gift of peace. It will be a peace that only God can give and it is called a perfect peace. You will find perfect peace and great calm and rest for your weary soul.

We keep that peace in our lives when we stay focused on God and his promises and not our situations. We keep his peace when we read his Word daily and call unto him in the wee hours of the morning and late at night. We have to learn to trust God because this is an essential key for the abiding peace.

We learn to trust God more and more when we allow him to take us through various adverse situations in life and we become fully aware that if it had not been for the Lord on our side, we would have been utterly consumed. We trust him over and over with our cares when he proves to us that he can and will handle them. He does it in such a way that we cannot deny that it was God that intervened on our behalf. It was him that blocked the enemy's assignment to destroy our life. Somebody ought to tell God thank you!

There will be times when you will be disappointed in the way God does a thing, but never throw your trust away. Remember, God knows what is best for you and he knows the way that he wants to bring you. We have to trust that God's love for us will not fail.

When we remember that our heavenly Father loves us so much that he gave his only Son for us and he will withhold no good thing from us, we become like a little child and we trust him. Roman 8:35 says, "Who shall separate us from the love of Christ? Shall tribulation, or distress, or persecution, or famine or nakedness, or peril, or sword?"

Verse twenty-seven says, "Nay in all these things we are more than conquerors through him that loved us."

Verse thirty-eight says, "For I am persuaded that neither death, or life nor angels nor principalities, nor powers nor things present, nor things to come, Nor height, nor depth nor any other creature, shall be able to separate us from the love of God which is in Christ Jesus our Lord."

This is a powerful passage because everything listed in these Scriptures would be a type of storm that a Christian would face, but through it all, God's love is there with us. Like the song says, if we never had a problem (storm), how would we know that God could solve it? How would we know just what God could do?

Our storms are sent to give us an experience with our God so that we will know him. The word bears witness because it says the people that know their God shall be strong and do exploits. We become strong when we allow God to develop our trust in him. We do the exploits because we know that it is him that empowers us to endure and overcome the obstacles and challenges of life.

I hope you are getting that we learn to trust in God by the things that we go through and when he brings us out safely a foundation of trust is built. He may not bring you out the way you want, but if you say like Christ, "Nevertheless not my will, but thine;" you will have peace and accept the will of God concerning you. Some things that God permits to come your way are working in you his divine purpose for your life. God has a purpose for our lives and our life is not over until that divine purpose is fulfilled.

> 2 Corinthians 1:9–10: For we would not, brethren, have you ignorant of our trouble which

came to us in Asia, that we were pressed out of measure, above strength, insomuch that we despaired even of life But we had the sentence of death in ourselves that we should not trust in ourselves, but in God which raises the dead. Who delivered us from so great a death and does deliver, in whom we trust that he will yet deliver us.

It is a good thing to trust in God. *Trust him!*

COMING THROUGH WITH OBEDIENCE

Another very important key to surviving our storm is obedience. I remember when Mount St. Helen was erupting, people were told to evacuate the mountain. There were those who wouldn't obey because they would not heed the warnings of those that were in authority. I have also seen when flooding is taking place in an area, there are those that will not leave their homes, even though they are told that the waters are rising and they need to leave the area. Some people are told that they need to board up the windows during hurricane and tornado seasons, and many follow direction and suffer minor loss of property, but many people don't follow instructions and suffer loss of property and life.

I thought of Paul, Acts 27:10, when he told those taking him to Rome, "Sirs I perceive that this voyage will be with hurt and much damage, not only of the lading and ship, but also of our lives." But the centurion and the master of the ship would not heed his warning and set sail anyway, and later there arose against it a tempestuous wind called Euroclydon.

Acts 27:14–15, and when the ship was caught, and could not bear up into the wind we let her drive. Act 27:31, Paul said to the centurion and to the soldiers, "Except these abide in the ship, ye cannot be saved."

The ship was being tossed back and forth by the fierce winds and many feared for their lives and wanted to abandon the ship. I don't know about you, but if I knew the ship was going to be destroyed, I think I would try to abandon that ship and take my chances in another boat. Isn't that the way it usually happens, when things are going bad in one place, we want to jump ship and get into another boat? People were panicking in the storm and they wanted to disobey and let down the other boats and jump in.

Sometimes all the signs point to abandon the ship, but if the Word comes to stay with the ship; the ship will be battered and worn and even destroyed, but if God said you shall live and not die, then obey and stay with the ship. God will bring you out safely. You might be battered and bruised, but nevertheless, you will be coming out.

> Acts 27:44: And the rest, some on boards, and some broken pieces of the ship. And so it came to pass that they escaped all safe to land.

You will escape destruction also if you learn to obey. Psalm 103:4 says, "Who redeemeth thy life from destruction, who crowneth thee with loving-kindness and tender mercies." Our heavenly Father requires obedience.

I thought of Jonah the prophet and his disobedience.

> Jonah 1:1–4: Now the word of the Lord came unto Jonah the son of Amittai saying, "Arise go to Nineveh, that great city, and cry against it for their wickedness is come up before me." But Jonah rose up to flee unto Tarshish from the presence of the Lord, and went down to Joppa and he found a ship going to Tarshish so he paid the fare thereof, and went down into it to go with them unto Tarshish from the presence of the Lord. But the Lord sent out a great wind into the sea and there was a mighty tempest in the sea, so that the ship was like to be broken.

God requires obedience from his people. Some storms arise in our lives to correct us when we are going in the wrong direction. God has to get our attention sometimes, so a great way to do this is by the circumstances and situations that arise in our life.

Jonah was going in the wrong direction. He was instructed to go to Nineveh and he went on the water way to Tarshish. His disobedience caused a great storm to arise in his life and in the life of the others that were on the ship. Storms just don't affect one household or one person. Disobeying God can cause many lives to be lost or a lot of negative things to flow into their life that they would not ordinarily have to face. We can't run or hide from the presence of God; he will deal with disobedience. As you can see to survive your storm you must heed warnings and you must learn to follow instructions.

The men on the ship sought their gods to find the reason this storm had arisen in their life and they cast forth the wares that were in the ship into the sea. They even asked Jonah to call upon his God so that he would think upon them and they would not perish. They discovered that Jonah was the reason for all troubles.

When you pray and God reveals to you why you are having a stormy life, and he tells you that if you will throw sin overboard you will have peace; then you must find out from him what the sin is and then throw it overboard. Can you give up that relationship that is robbing you of the will of God in your life? He looks good and he seems to be the man you have been waiting on. But there is one problem: he is not saved.

Can you stop spending more than you make so that your financial life can run a smooth course? Maybe you are having a financial crisis because you are trying to live beyond your means to keep up with the Jones. When he says cut the credit cards up; then cut them up. When he says pay tithes and offerings; that is what he means. He wants to bless you in your finances, but he can't go against his Word. You must learn to throw disobedience overboard to survive your storm.

Like those mariners on the ship to Tarshish; we must see, God to find out the reason and the solution to our storms. *Throw it overboard!* Hebrew 12:1 says it this way, "Wherefore seeing we also are compassed about with so great a cloud of witnesses, let us lay aside every weight, and the sin which doth so easily beset us, and let us run with patience the race that is set before us." Just like there are things that hinder a runner and prevent him from winning the race; there are things that will weigh you down and prevent you from coming through your storm. God wants you to *lay them aside! Better yet, throw it overboard!*

WAITING OUT THE STORM

The last key that I have for you is a very important one, but it is often the key that we don't like to use. In this age of instant coffee, instant pudding, instant cake, and the microwave and jets that are almost as fast as the speeding bullet; we have been conditioned to think that everything should happen quickly.

We act fast and we discard everything that may slow us down. We want quick solutions to our problems, quick answers to our questions and prayers, quick food, quick travel, quick homes. Yes, even building a home is quick these days, all you have to do is lay the foundation and someone will bring you the house in parts and nail it together. You will have a house in days instead of months. We want what we want; how we want it and when we want it and usually the when is now ASAP.

I have discovered that you may be able to hurry man, but you cannot hurry God. God will do what he wants when he wants and how he wants. God has his own timing and he won't be hurried by man.

The problem is that every time we use our microwave, cook instant food, take fast jets, and build pre-fabricated homes, we are being robbed of our ability to wait. God is a longsuffering God, and he waited a long time for some of us to repent and to turn to him. Since God is not a hurry-up God, and we want to be in harmony with God, we will have to renew our mind and learn how to wait on the Lord.

God can appear to be slow according to human time, but we are not to become discouraged and give up. It is good to know that while we are waiting God will strengthen our heart so that we will be able to endure until he moves in our situation according to human time, but we are not to become discouraged and give up. It is good to know that while we are waiting, God will strengthen our heart so that we will be able to endure until he moves in our situation, as we hope in him and how he has purposed for our life.

The Bible says in Psalm 27:13–14:

> I had fainted, unless I had believed to see the goodness of the Lord in the land of the living. Wait on the Lord be of good courage, and he shall strengthen thine heart, wait, I say, on the Lord.
>
> Isaiah 40:31: But they that wait upon the Lord shall renew their strength; they shall mount up with wings as eagles; they shall run,

and not be weary, and they shall walk, and not faint.

God will give you power and he will not allow you to quit. While we are waiting for God to divinely intervene in our affairs; we want to make sure that we keep the right attitude and not murmur or complain. This is how you should wait for the promise of God to be fulfilled in your life:

Wait patiently and quietly
Wait courageously
Wait confidently
Wait expectantly

If we don't learn how to wait on God, we can miss our blessing and destiny. Satan will rob us of what God had in store for us and give us something else.

Wait patiently and quietly. We are not to be anxious and have worry-itis. God's promises are sure and amen. Get somewhere and sit down have some coffee or drink some tea. Don't prance back in forth wearing out your carpet. Wait on him; he is moving in ways that you don't understand and in ways that you can't see right now. While you are drinking your coffee or tea, don't pick up that telephone and call another person and start murmuring and complaining about your situation and allowing doubt and unbelief to enter your spirit. *Be quiet. Now receive the peace of God.*

When we wait courageously on the Lord, he will supernaturally equip us with strength. We will be like that energized bunny; instead of fainting or giving out, we will keep on going because our focus will be God instead of our problem. We will be able to rest and not be distracted when it seems that others are moving ahead of us or prospering when we are barely getting by. We will have boldness and power to forge ahead and face any storm we are confronted with. Just to know that God is with us brings power to the soul.

When I think of the word expectantly, it brings to mind Psalm 62:5 which says, "My soul, wait thou only upon God for my expectation is from him."

Hope and expectation go together; for if you have a hope, then naturally you are expecting some type of change to manifest in your situation and that expectation was placed in your heart by God. You are waiting and expecting him to come with healing, salvation, deliverance, or financial blessing. Keep waiting and expecting and God will show up. He will not disappoint or make ashamed.

After you have gone through and you have survived your storm, now you can be a witness for God. God needs a true witness. Now you can tell your story and you can tell about the goodness of God. You can tell exactly how he brought you out. You can tell how he helped you and how he didn't leave you and how he provided for you. You can even tell how it wasn't easy and there were many a days and many a nights that you wanted to give up, but God stepped in right on time and strengthened you just when you were about to blow it.

Now that you have been helped; you can help somebody. Now that you have been comforted; you can comfort somebody. *Go through; God needs a witness!*

I hope that this little book will inspire someone to keep on pressing on and in the words of Helen Keller, "The best way out is always through."

The Spirit of the Lord is still saying, *"Go through my child, go through"*